How to teach poetry writing at key stage 2

MICHAELA MORGAN

David Fulton Publishers

David Fulton Publishers Ltd
Ormond House, 26-27 Boswell Street, London, WC1N 3JZ

www.fultonpublishers.co.uk

First published in Great Britain by David Fulton Publishers 2001
Reprinted 2002

British Library Publication Data
A catalogue record for this book is available from the British Library

ISBN 1-85346-804-5

Also available in the **Writers' Workshop Series:**

How to teach writing across the curriculum at key stage 2   ISBN 1-85346-803-7
How to teach fiction writing at key stage 2   ISBN 1-85346-833-9

Edited by Dodi Beardshaw
Designed by Ken Vail Graphic Design
Illustrations by Martin Cater
Cover photographs by John Redman
Typeset by FiSH Books, London
Printed in Great Britain by Bell and Bain Ltd, Glasgow

Contents

Acknowledgements

Acknowledgements are due to the following copyright holders, for permission to reproduce poems:

Roger McGough, for 'The Sound Collector', from *Pillow Talk*, Viking 1990, reprinted by permission of Penguin Group Ltd.

Carol Ann Duffy, for 'Three', from *Hello New*, Orchard Books, 2000, © Carol Ann Duffy.

Valerie Bloom for 'December', from *Let Me Touch the Sky*, Macmillan Children's Books 2000, © Valerie Bloom.

Chatto & Windus for 'Mama Dot' by Fred D'Aguiar, from *Mama Dot* published by Chatto & Windus. Used by permission of the Random House Group Limited.

While the publishers have made every effort to contact copyright holders of previously published material in this volume, they would be grateful to hear from any they were unable to contact.

I would like to acknowledge the help and inspiration of the poems, books and workshops of the following:

John Cotton
Roger McGough
Brian Patten
Kit Wright
Sandy Brownjohn

Writers' Workshop

Writers' Workshop

A scribble of writers scrabbling for new
    ways,
Crossing out and changing, making blots of
    mistakes.
Herd of oxymoron in the background
    brightly snoring.
A litter of alliteration on the look out,
    lying low.
A chorus could come in, chanting,
    chanting.
A repeated refrain here and there, here and
    there.
Metaphors are matadors, they add their
    flourishes,
Similes wait like actors in the wings.
A scribble of writers now searching for an
    ending.
A question? Or a shock! Or a gentle fade...
Reach for the tools to hammer out those
    sentences.
A workshop of writing waiting to be made.

Michaela Morgan

Making a start

Reading, hearing and enjoying poetry

Regularly read poetry aloud to your class and to yourself – just for the poem, not for any follow-up work or to make any point. *Poem for the Day* or a good anthology (such as *The Puffin Book of Twentieth-Century Children's Verse*) will provide a wealth of varied poetry. Reading one of these just before a break, or to start or finish the day, will not eat into your time and will help hone the ear and increase the breadth of acquaintance with poetry. The book should be readily available for those who want to reread the day's poem.

Encourage children to find favourite poems and read them aloud to you, the class, or each other. Enjoy the music of language as well as its meaning.

Honing the ear and all the senses

From time to time, take a few moments to listen or stand and stare. Ask the class to note down what you and they can see, hear, touch, taste or smell and try to find a descriptive word or a simile to capture these observations. Complete silence in the classroom is necessary for the listening time. Silence is 'when you hear things'. Note the smallest of noises – also what you imagine you can hear (e.g. *I hear a ticking, tick tick tick – the clock or the teacher's pen or the brain clicking as it thinks*). Teachers should join in this activity – to be seen quietly concentrating, scribbling, crossing out, etc. provides a good role model – plus you'll enjoy the activity.

Making a word hoard and writing together

Gather words and ideas in a whole-class or group session. Jot down all suggestions on a flip chart or board, and link words which go together because of their rhyme, alliteration, etc. Compose whole-class poems together before considering sending children off to write individually. Sometimes, take existing poems and omit words or phrases. Discuss which would be good words or phrases to insert.

Reading aloud

Reading aloud is an excellent chance to hear how/if a poem is working. This is a time to consider making changes. The plenary is a good opportunity to hear rough drafts, applaud them and consider revisions.

Redrafting and revising

The first writing of a poem is a beginning. Changes and improvements can be made. Do whole-class or group redrafting sessions on whole-class poems. Demonstrate the process of crossing out and changing, discussing reasons for the changes. Things to consider here are: deleting unnecessary words (poetry is economical); changing words for onomatopoeic, alliterative, or other more powerful words; tightening rhythm or rhyme; altering word order to put emphasis on important words or to avoid having to stretch for a rhyme; punctuating.

Being more specific and detailed can help a poem. Instead of *we sat under a tree*, consider what sort of tree. *We sat under the willow* or *we sat under the oak?*

Poetry is less painful than a story to redraft. Writing poetry encourages experimentation with word choice, word order, etc.

Making a collection

Making a class anthology is a wonderfully useful and enjoyable activity. You can choose a theme or poetic form or just let children find any poem they like. They copy their poem out (or key it in). Copying a poem sharpens the understanding of the poem. You often notice much more about a piece when you have to write it exactly as the poet has written it. Why is that punctuation there? Why is that line broken here? Each child can read his or her chosen poem aloud and try to explain what they like about it. Some children could learn their poem by heart. The heart is a good place to keep a poem.

Punctuation

Inviting a poet

Consider inviting a poet to school. Try for a poet whose work you have enjoyed – approach him or her through the publisher. The children can then hear a poem in the poet's voice and talk about it. Maybe the poet will run a workshop or sign copies of his or her books. Prepare for the visit and follow it up. Allow children who can to buy copies of the books – to make the poems their own. If this is difficult, then you should ensure the poems are bought and available to all in the library or classroom.

Tools of the trade

Make sure you have:

improving vocabulary)

- a rhyming dictionary (Penguin publish a good one)
- a thesaurus (again Penguin publish an excellent thesaurus – Roget's, or you may prefer to opt for a thesaurus specifically targeted at children)
- a large and good selection of books of poetry, including rhyming and unrhyming, and classic and contemporary.

And finally . . .

Why write poetry?

The skills involved in writing poetry are transferable to all types of writing. All writing benefits from careful word choice, detail, keen observation, use of the senses, thoughtfulness, and awareness. Word games and verse hone specific writing skills. Poetry requires revisions and redraftings. All writers, particularly young ones, can become downhearted at revising longer pieces of writing but the brevity and focus of poetry makes writing appealing, acheivable and fun. Poetry is playful – it encourages experimentation.

A to Z of Poetry

A

Acrostic

A very popular poetic form in schools. The title of the poem (e.g. 'Holiday') is written vertically and provides the initial for each line:

H
O
L
I
D
A
Y

If you are going to write an acrostic, do some examples as a whole-class activity first and demonstrate the gathering of ideas before writing each line. Consider what makes a holiday, for example resting, lying in bed late, sunny days, ice cream and lollies, taking it easy, etc. Then try to include some of the things you want to say in the acrostic:

> **Happiness is our hope**
> **On our holidays.**
> **Lying in bed all day,**
> **Idling, lazing, dreaming**
> **Dozing...**
> **All the time in the world**
> **Yes!**

Advertisement poem

Advertising agencies think very carefully about their advertisements. Some of them have poetic qualities (rhyme, rhythm, alliteration and onomatopoeia are particularly popular devices). Look at advertisements, then try writing ones that tempt the reader to eat oranges, go swimming, read a book, etc.

Alliteration

Words beginning with the same sound (not necessarily the same letter – as in *free phone* or *one wonderful wombat*). Used frequently and to enormous effect by the Anglo-Saxons (see Appendix for examples), alliteration remains widely used today in poetry and song. It is an effective way of binding words together and making music with words.

Alphabet poem

Take a subject and write an A to Z of it. For example, if you were to take 'Cat' as your subject, you could write a poem composed of adjectives:

> **Athletic, balletic, cosy cat.**
> **Daring, energetic, furry cat.**

Or verbs:

> **I am Cat.**
> **I attack, I bite, I curl, I dance...**

Ambiguity

Deliberate ambiguity – an excellent device in poetry. Unintentional ambiguity (*the secretary went down to the kitchen and brought up her dinner*) can have quite a different effect.

Assonance

Subtler than rhyming, it is a repetition of sounds to make a half rhyme, e.g. *crying time*.

B

Ballad

The ballads of Robin Hood or *Sir Patrick Spens* are examples of traditional ballads. They tell a story in a regular, usually four-lined ('quatrain'), form with a regular rhyme scheme (typically *abba*). A modern example of a ballad is 'Timothy Winters' by Charles Causley.

Brainstorming

When brainstorming for words, accept all offerings and note them. Then select from those words submitted, giving reasons for your choice, e.g. 'This has a sharp sound' or 'I like the alliteration here'.

C

Calligram

The formation of the characters, or the font, represents something of the word's meaning (e.g.

SHOUT! or *whisper*). See workshops 5 and 6: 'Waves' and 'Space Rap'.

Cinquain

Having 5 lines and a total of 22 syllables, in the sequence 2, 4, 6, 8, 2, this form was invented by an American who called herself a 'poetess'. I am unaware of any outstanding poems written in this form, but it is suggested in the framework! As a cinquain is essentially a 'building-up' poem, try a shopping poem – starting off, collecting more and more things, collapsing and returning home. Or try a racing, or a sports day, poem.

Concrete poem

Another term for a **Shape poem**. See Workshop 5: 'Waves'.

Confidence

An essential! Try not to be tempted into decrying even 'silly' or 'rude' suggestions during brainstorming times. Out of mischief, creativity can creep. Acknowlege successful poems – or lines or even words. Be tactful with revision suggestions.

Conversational

Many, or rather most, poems are in a particular poet's voice, as if the poet is having a conversation with you. Read Michael Rosen's work for examples of work which captures rhythms and vocabulary of everyday language, situations and conversation.

Couplet

Two consecutive rhyming lines. See Workshops 1 and 2: 'Monday's Child' and 'The Day the Zoo Escaped'.

D

Dialogue

Don't forget that dialogue can be included in poems: in fact, entire poems have been made of dialogue. Try 'Ghosts' by Kit Wright in *Rabbiting On*, published by Young Lions.

Diary poem

Try a diary of a goldfish – plenty of scope for repetition, refrain and changing word order to make slight differences!

E

Elegy

A lament, usually for the loss or death of someone. Try an elegy to a favourite teddy or to a lost sock.

Empathy

To stand in the shoes of someone else, and imagine and write how it would feel. Poetry taps into the imagination, creativity and empathy of human beings in a way that transcends anything you can target in the National Literacy Strategy.

Epic

A long story or poem of heroic endevour. Not to be attempted seriously in class unless you have a year or two, maybe a decade, to spare!

Epitaph

An attempt to sum up a life in a few words. An epitaph usually starts with *Here lies...* You will find a wealth of them in *The Faber Book of Epigrams and Epitaphs*, where you will note that they often use wordplay to humorous or critical effect. The Earl of Rochester's epitaph on King Charles II is fairly typical:

> **Here lies our Sovereign Lord, the King,**
> **Whose word no man relies on;**
> **Who never said a foolish thing,**
> **Nor ever did a wise one.**

Probably best attempted as the summation of the life of a typical figure (e.g. a figure representing a profession, such as a teacher), rather than of an individual. They can be cruel as in one I prepared earlier:

> **Here lies a footballer**
> **whistle blown on his last game.**
> **He kicked the bucket, not the ball,**
> **and was never seen again.**

F

Figurative language

Use of simile, metaphor and similar devices.

Form

Providing a form for writers to follow can provide a release and a starting point for writing – but feel free to adapt the form. It should be a supporting framework, not a straitjacket. Don't let unfamiliarity with poetic forms intimidate you – if you want examples of every poetic form, use Frances Stillman's *The Poet's Manual and Rhyming Dictionary*, published by Thames and Hudson.

Free verse

Verse freed from the need to rhyme – which has words carefully chosen for other reasons than rhyme.

G

Have a GO!

Poetry is all around us and is one thing everyone can have a go at. Even those who 'don't like writing' can love poetry – though they may not know it. Anyone who can enjoy wordplay in jokes, or who enjoys rhythm and sound in music, anyone like this can write a poem – and enjoy it!

H

Haiku

A traditional Japanese form of poem which encourages a careful and economical choice of words, based on an awareness of syllables. Every word counts in a haiku. Every line break has to be carefully considered. A very brief form, it can help jolt a writer away from usual rhythms, pounding rhymes and well-used vocabulary. It is an exercise in making restrained choices with language. See also Workshop 3: 'Haiku'.

A haiku always has 17 syllables. It consists of three lines only. Line one has five syllables, line two has seven, and the third and last line has five. A brief moment in time is captured in a clear visual image. *The Penguin Book Of Japanese Verse* provides many examples. See also **Tanka**.

I

Idiom

Everyday figures of speech (see Appendix: 'Figuratively Speaking'). Not to be taken literally!

Images

Use of language to capture or create a mental picture of something.

Internal rhyme

Rhyme within a line, as in *You peel and you grapple with orange or apple*. Internal rhyme can also be within a word, as in *hubbub*.

J

Jokes

Jokes and wordplay alert us to language. Jokes can rely on puns, homophones, spoonerisms, etc., for their effect. They, and tongue-twisters too, are little steps towards poetry.

K

Kenning

Found in Norse and Old English poetry a kenning is similar to a riddle, as the thing described is not named but described in compound expressions, usually of two words (e.g. *fast forgetter* or *ankle-biter*). See also Workshop 4: 'Fin Flapper'.

L

Letter poem

Blythely mentioned in the National Literacy Strategy – but are there any good examples of letter poems? If you know one, let me know! See also **Renga**.

Limerick

A light-hearted exercise best done as a group or class activity. The finest examples are probably those of Edward Lear. The famed *Anon.* also produces a remarkably large quantity of limericks!

Line breaks

It's worth taking a well-known poem and writing it out as continuous prose. Then, with the class, have a go at breaking it into lines. This is the best way of alerting an apprentice writer to the choices and possibilities line breaks provide.

List poem

Think of a subject and list its qualities:

Christmas is...
dark nights
bright lights
rising hopes
etc.

Other possible subjects: *The contents of my head are...; In my pencil case...* Encourage children to put unexpected, witty or well-described things in their lists. If they keep to a carefully controlled number of words in each line, they have a **Thin poem** too! (See entry below.)

M

Metaphor

A figure of speech in which one thing is said to be another. An example of this is in the poem 'Writers' Workshop' on page 5: *Metaphors are matadors, they add their flourishes...* See also Workshop 7: 'I am a Baggy Tee Shirt'.

Monologue

A poem can be written as a monologue – one person, or one animal, or one object talking.

N

Narrative poem

A narrative poem tells a story. Ballads are narrative poems. See Workshop 13: 'The Dead Quire'.

Near rhyme

Near or half rhyme can give wider choice and subtler effect than full rhyme, e.g. *summer/dimmer*.

Ngu Utu

A Japanese form of poetry which alternates lines of 5 and 7 syllables in a poem of any length, ending with two rhyming lines of 7 syllables.

Nonsense poem

Nonsense poems are wonderfully liberating. I suggest 'Jabberwocky' by Lewis Carroll, who invented portmanteau words in this tour de force. Also read poems by Spike Milligan.

O

Observation poem

Based on observation. Take the time to stand and stare – to really look, hear, taste, smell and feel...

Onomatopoeia

An interesting word in itself! Made up of two Greek words for 'name' and 'make'. Words, like *hiss*, that make the sound they are describing are onomatopoeic. See Workshop 8: 'The Sound Collector'.

Oral poetry

Children will be acquainted with a range of oral poetry which they can be reminded of – jingles, playing songs, nursery rhymes. All poetry was once oral – epics and ballads were composed as poetry to make them more memorable before writing became widespread. The oral tradition continues strongly today.

Oxymoron

An apparent contradiction as in *bitter-sweet* or *gloomily gambolling*. There is an example (*brightly snoring*) in the poem 'Writers' Workshop' on page 5.

P

Personification

Language that gives non-human things and objects human emotions or attributes, e.g. *The trees dripped with sadness...* See Workshop 9: 'Nocturnophobia'.

Poem

A poem is many, many things, some of them contradictory. It can be direct – a quick connection to the heart, the memories, the senses. It can be indirect, subtly hinting. It can be moving, mysterious, sad, serious, comic, crazy, funny. It can be downright nonsense. It can explode. It can whisper. You can join in and clap and sing or whisper it softly in your own quiet mind.

Coleridge defined a poem as 'the best words in the best order'. Wordsworth described his work as 'a selection of the real language of men in a state of vivid sensation'. In a poem, language is used with awareness but should be real. Pope's famous adage 'What oft was said but ne'er so well expressed' sums it up. It's not just what you say but how you say it. Poetry is generally (but not necessarily) economical with language. The main thing – it is a source of delight!

Q

Quatrain

A four-line stanza.

Question-and-answer poem

Ask everyone to write a question (a wide-ranging one such as *What is the sun?*) Then try to answer the questions – not factually!

R

Rap

A form of oral poetry which has a very strong rhythm and regular rhyme. See Workshop 6: 'Space Rap'.

Recipe poem

A poem which imitates the form of a recipe. See Appendix: 'Recipe for a Story'.

Refrain

A repeated line, or group of lines, in a poem can help to bind it together. See Workshop 12: 'Hubble Bubble'.

Renga

A series of haiku each linked to the next by two seven-syllable lines. Sometimes a poet would write a haiku and send it to another poet, who would link it and add his or her own haiku – making a sort of letter poem. See also Workshop 3: 'Haiku'.

Rhyme

The reading of poetry of all sorts will demonstrate that it doesn't have to rhyme. That said, rhyme does have an enormous attraction. *But* if you are in danger of being forced into writing something pointless or silly, something that breaks the mood or lets the poem down – abandon the rhyme. The poem should say what we want it to say – rhyme is an extra.

Rhythm

All poetry has some sort of rhythm – which is not to say it necessarily has a regular thumping rhythm. Sometimes an irregular, subtle rhythm or cadence is much more suitable to the mood of a poem.

Riddles

A great tradition spanning *The Exeter Book* (Old English poetry) to the *Beano*. W. H. Auden memorably wrote that 'one of the elements of poetry is the riddle. You do not call a spade a spade.'

S

Shape poem

A poem whose words are laid out in a way that reflects the subject. Also called **Concrete poem**. See Workshop 5: 'Waves'.

Simile

A figure of speech in which one thing is said to be like (or as) another. See the example in the poem 'Writers' Workshop' on page 5: *Similes wait like actors in the wings.*

Stanza

The approved word to use for what is often referred to as a 'verse'!

T

Tanka

An extended form of haiku consisting of 5 lines and a total of 31 syllables, in the sequence 5, 7, 5, 7, 7. One of the great masters of tanka was Ki Tsurayuki. Here is a translation of one he wrote nearly a thousand years ago:

> **When I went to see,**
> **That winter, my much loved girl,**
> **The night wind blew**
> **So cold against the river**
> **That the water birds were crying.**

It is a word picture similar to a haiku but its extended form means it can also have some story element.

Thin poem

One or two words per line – set an arbitrary limit and stick to it. See also **List poem**.

U

Understanding

'But what does it *mean*?' Sometimes you cannot completely explain the meaning of a poem. That's part of the point of poetry – it has meanings behind and beyond its initial meaning. Sometimes just let a poem wash over you – don't try to understand it, just enjoy the sounds, the mood. The understanding of it might creep up on you bit by bit over time...

V

Verse

Often used to mean stanza (as in 'the poem has four verses') but properly used to mean something slightly less than poetry. I write verse and sometimes I write poetry – sometimes my writing has the higher attributes of poetry – sometimes it has the rhyme, rhythm, etc. associated with poetry but it is of a lesser order.

Voice

Poems gain strength from being written in the poet's particular voice – the poet's own individual way of expressing himself or herself with words, images and language that are real and rooted in the poet's own life. See Workshop 11: 'December'. Allow children to use their everyday language within their poems. Poetry should not be kept on a pedestal.

W

Wordgames

Free the mind, focus on a skill, or start the creative process by playing a word game. Excellent ideas can be found in *Word Games* by Sandy Brownjohn and Janet Whitaker, published by Hodder and Stoughton.

Writing frame

I've provided some for you; alternatively, you can make your own by taking a poem and blanking out a word (or words), a line, a simile. Do a line from time to time just as a quick activity. Take 'I wandered lonely as a cloud' and try as:

I _____ lonely as a _____.

X

Excitement! Exultation! Exhilaration! Exclamations! and now... Exiting from the need to find something beginning with X.

Y

Yes! Yippee and Yabbadabadoo! Feeling positive...feeling confident...having fun with words...writing a poem with...

Z

Zest and zip and ZING!

Monday's Child

Monday's child is fair of face.

Tuesday's child is full of grace.

Wednesday's child is full of woe.

Thursday's child has far to go.

Friday's child is loving and giving.

Saturday's child works hard for a living

but the child that is born on the Sabbath day

is bonny and blythe and good and gay.

Anon. trad.

Monday's Child

Key concepts

Rhyming couplets
Poems from different cultures and times
Language changes over time
Traditional and modern poetry
Half rhyme/near rhyme.

Read! Speak! Listen! Enjoy!

- Photocopy and enlarge the poem so that the whole class can see it.
- Read the verse aloud. Different readers read.

Discuss

- Who wrote this poem? How old do you think it is? Did you already know it? Point out how much poetry we know without realising it, e.g. nursery rhymes and the oral tradition, jingles and songs...
- What clues can you find to the age of the poem? (Subject matter, style, form, words used, anonymous author, traditional.)
- Vocabulary: some of the words used in this verse are localised, antiquated, or have changed their meaning over the years. Explain *Sabbath* ('Sunday' – or 'Saturday' in the Jewish tradition, but this verse is probably Scots or Northern English), *bonny* ('good-looking', 'beautiful'), *gay* ('happy', 'light-hearted' – this is the original meaning of gay which is now changing its meaning). Some of these words are still in current use in different parts of the country and in different communities.
- Discuss the form of this verse. It is in rhyming couplets. Identify the couplets and the rhyme scheme.
- Find examples of alliteration.

Analyse model

- The verse goes through the days of the week in turn, has a regular rhythm (beat it out) and rhyme scheme, and is easily memorable.
- Discuss the use of a description like *fair of face*. Why would the verse be less effective if the line was *Monday's child is pretty*?

✎ Write

- **Whole-class activity: write a poem modelled on this one.**
  - Teacher as scribe, taking suggestions from the class and modelling the process of brainstorming, note-jotting, rough writing, choosing, changing...
  - In the class poem, aim to use the language of today – write a modern-day version.
  - Encourage the use of dictionary and thesaurus to find alternative words.
  - Here's one idea:

Monday's child plays in the rain.
Tuesday's child is such a pain.
Wednesday's child is very cheeky.
Thursday's child is somewhat sneaky.
Friday's child is speedy and sporty.
Saturday's child is rather naughty
but the child that is born on the Sabbath day
is as bad as the rest. It's true. OK!

- **Move on to independent work.**
  - Children can move on to writing their own individual poems based on the model and the whole-class poem.
  - Children who need support for this activity can be given a writing frame – with as many gaps in it as you feel appropriate. You may include some rhymes to help out:

Monday's child stays in bed

Wednesday's child is lazy too

Friday's child screams and screams

---

but the child that is born on the Sabbath day

Rhymes: has a pain in the head/turns bright red/cries boo hoo/scoffs bowls of stew/loves ice-creams/has bad dreams.

Perform! Discuss! Enjoy! Applaud!

Plenary and revision/redrafting

- Read out and comment on particularly good choices of words.
- Make the point that poems are worked and reworked. Can anyone suggest improvements or alternatives?
- Incorporate revisions.
- Ask children to write or type out their lines, with revisions incorporated.
- Present as a collection in Big Book or display format.

Possibilities for follow-up

- Look at the poem 'Mama Dot' by Fred D'Aguiar (see Appendix). This Guyanan-born writer has used what was a light-hearted framework to make a deeper poem. The poem tells the story of those who were taken from their homes in Ashante and sold into slavery in the nineteenth century.
- Compare the two poems.
  - D'Aguiar's poem is also in couplets. Find the rhymes. Point out that the poet uses half rhyme or near rhyme as well as full rhyme.
  - It also goes through the days of the week. The poet uses this as a way of telling a life story: the days of the week are metaphorical, not literal, days.
  - The original 'Monday's Child' verse uses words which are rooted in a particular time, place and culture. D'Aguiar's poem is rooted in his tradition, history, language and culture.
  - D'Aguiar's poem is written in a particular 'voice'. It sounds as if the story is being told to us by someone who understands, who 'speaks the same language'. This directness adds to its power, making it more memorable. If the poet had used more formal language and a more complex form, what effect would this have?
- Children can try writing a life-story poem on D'Aguiar's model.

Objectives

This workshop is relevant to many year groups, particularly for the following objectives.

Y3T2 oral and performance poetry from other cultures Text 4, 5, 11: choose and prepare poems for performance; rehearse and improve performance; write new or extended verses for performance.

Y4T1 Text 7, 14: compare/contrast poems on similar themes; write poems based on experience; Word 13, 15, 16: use rhyming dictionary; joined handwriting; informal/neat writing.

Y4T2 poems from different cultures and times Text 5, 6, 7, 11: figurative language; archaic words; patterns of rhyme and verse; write poetry based on structure/style of poems read; Word 11: vocabulary changes over time.

Y4T3 raising issues Text 4, 5, 6, 7, 14, 15: poetic terms; count syllables; rhyme structures; forms/uses of poetry; write poems with different styles/structures; produce polished poetry through revision.

The Day the Zoo Escaped

The day the zoo escaped...

the zebras zipped out quickly,
the snakes slid out slickly,

the lions marched out proudly,
the hyenas laughed out loudly,

the mice skipped out lightly,
the parrots flew out brightly,

but the hippopotomus,
stubbornly,

just stayed where it was.

Michaela Morgan and Sue Palmer

The Day the Zoo Escaped

Key concepts

Redrafting
Encouraging use of powerful verbs
Synonyms.

Read! Speak! Listen! Enjoy!

- Photocopy and enlarge the poem so that the whole class can see it.
- Read the verse aloud. Different readers read, either individually or in groups.
- Encourage reading with expression – a different voice for *loudly, proudly, skipped, marched,* etc.
- Enjoy!

Discuss

- What form does this poem take? Does it rhyme? (Apart from the introductory line and the final line, the poem is written in rhyming couplets. Find the couplets.)
- Can you find any alliteration in the poem?

Analyse model

Consider and discuss the choice of words. Emphasise the range of synonyms for *went* or *walked.*

✎ Write

- **Whole-class activity: revise and redraft the poem.**
  - Using the writing frame provided at the end of this workshop and acting as scribe, substitute more vigorous verbs for *went* and a variety of adverbs for *quickly.* The words do not have to rhyme, but they can if you wish. You could write the main body of the poem in couplets.
  - Make a list of words you might consider using. (Some helpful words: *slithered, slid, rushed, charged, climbed, clambered, crept, scuttled, tiptoed, hurried, hopped, wandered, inched, scurried, shuffled, chased, ran; cheekily, scarily, creepily, bouncily, happily, sheepishly, sluggishly, slothfully, lazily, sleepily, rapidly, racily, sneakily, snakily, shakily, hastily.*)
  - Encourage the use of dictionary and thesaurus.

- **Independent work: write a poem based on the same model.**
  - Animals you might suggest using: wolves, eagles, tigers, bears, crocodiles, snakes, bats, wildcats, hippos, elephants, slugs, snakes, tortoises, etc.
  - You can substitute *slowly* (and synonyms for *slowly*) for *quickly.*

Perform! Discuss! Enjoy! Applaud!

Plenary and revision/redrafting

- Read out and comment on particularly good choices of words.
- Make the point that poems are worked and reworked. Can anyone suggest improvements or alternatives?
- Incorporate revisions.
- Ask children to write or type out their lines – with revisions incorporated.
- Present as a collection in Big Book or display format.

Possibilities for follow-up

Write a poem using an adverb at the beginning, rather than the end, of each line:

Quietly the...

Silently the...

(As in the James Reeves poem 'Slowly the tide creeps up the sand'.)

Objectives

This workshop is relevant to many year groups, particularly for the following objectives.

Y3T1 Text 6, 9, 12: recite poems and discuss choice of words; generate ideas through brainstorming; collect suitable words/phrases for writing poems.

Y3T2 Text 4, 5: choose and prepare poems for performance; rehearse and improve performance.

Y4T1 Sentence 3, 4: identify the use of powerful verbs; identify adverbs and understand their function; use adverbs with greater discrimination in own writing; Text 14: write poems based on experience, linked to poems read.

Y4T2 Text 7: identify different patterns of rhyme and verse in poetry.

Writing frame

Revise! Redraft! Improve!

The Day the Zoo Escaped

The day the zoo escaped...

the monkeys went out quickly,
the spiders went out quickly,

the tigers went out quickly,
the rabbits went out quickly,

the rats went out quickly,
the cheetah went out quickly,
but the sloth,
        sleepily,
                just hung around.

Haiku

1

Over the doorway
The ivy creeps in the light
Of evening's moon.

Matsuo Basho 1644-94

2

The grasshopper's cry
Does not reveal how very
Soon they are to die.

Matsuo Basho 1644-94

3

Beat This!

Every word counts
in a Japanese haiku
Try one for yourself!

Michaela Morgan

4

Taking Flight

Haiku haiku hai
haiku haiku haiku ku
first haiku of Spring!

Michaela Morgan

5

A Splashing Time!

Splattering rain drops
puddles grow into small ponds
Hopeful ducks are gathering.

Michaela Morgan

Every Word Counts

Key concepts

Careful word choice
Syllable counting
Line breaks
Classic and modern poetry
Producing polished poetry through revision, deletion, reorganisation.

Read! Speak! Listen! Enjoy!

- Photocopy and enlarge the poems so that the whole class can see them.
- Read the poems aloud several times. Different readers read.
- Discuss the best ways of reading these. Taking your time to read the traditional haiku is essential – otherwise one gulp and it's gone. This will encourage children to perform their own work with care.
- With the two traditional haiku, read slowly and allow words to linger in the air. The light-hearted ones need a more throwaway style of performance. A group can read 'Taking Flight', making it sound like a cuckoo call in Spring.
- Enjoy!

Discuss

- What do you notice about these poems? Ensure that the children realise that each set of three lines is a separate and individual poem.
- The length of the poems – they can be very short. A haiku is just three lines long.
- The lack of rhyme. A poem has carefully chosen words – sometimes the words are chosen to rhyme, sometimes they are chosen for their meaning, sometimes for their sound/music or alliteration. In this case, they have been chosen for their meaning and for the number of syllables in each word.
- Remind the children what a syllable is. Practise counting beats by tapping out the children's names or very familiar words. Clap the beats to *Tom, Kerry, playground, December.*
- Count the beats in the words of the model poems. Mark the syllables in each word. Explain that a haiku is an old Japanese form of verse which always has five syllables in the first line, seven syllables in the second, and five syllables in the last line.
- Haiku are usually snapshot word pictures

which try to capture a moment in time.
- They encourage the writer to choose words carefully – to search for alternative words and be aware of syllables. They encourage writing with care – every word counts. Unnecessary words can be deleted (this is good practice for all poetry writing).

Analyse models

- The traditional Japanese models both describe nature and a particular time. The final line of a haiku often offers a sense of conclusion.
- Modern haiku is often more playful than traditional Japanese haiku, but still preserves the syllable count and the three-line form.
- Traditional haiku offers a calm, thoughtful mood. How does it achieve this? (By lack of pounding rhythm and rhyme which would increase pace and take away from the contemplative quality of the poem.)
- Notice in haiku 1 that the definite article (*the*) before *evening's* has been omitted – why? Comment how often poetry is trimmed down to its essentials. A poet will revise a poem and delete.
- Notice the line endings in haiku 2. A poet chooses carefully where to start and end each line. Why has the poet ended the lines where he does?
- The three modern examples have added a title. The title does not just repeat the content of the verse – it tries to add something to it.

✍ Write

- **Whole-class activity: write a haiku.**
  - Teacher as scribe.
  - Encourage the use of dictionary and thesaurus to find alternative words.
  - Subjects might include: a view out of the window (a word picture of something seen); a season; an animal or bird; a type of weather. Select a subject and gather words and ideas.What could you say about the subject?
  - Rough-draft the first line. Then reduce or extend it to the right number of syllables. You may have to add a word or take words away. You may have to change the line breaks. You may have to revise vocabulary – finding alternative words with different syllable counts.

– Demonstrate crossing out, reading out, checking and changing as part of the writing process. Encourage syllable counting and careful word choice. Encourage the finding of a title – one that does not simply repeat the subject of the poem but somehow adds to it.

- **Move on to independent work.** Children's haiku can be thematically linked – each taking a month to make a haiku calendar or each taking a colour to make a haiku rainbow.

Perform! Discuss! Enjoy! Applaud!

Plenary and revision/redrafting

- Read out and comment on particularly good choices of words.
- Make the point that poems are worked and reworked. Can anyone suggest improvements or alternatives?
- Incorporate revisions.
- Ask children to write or type out their lines – with revisions incorporated.
- Present as a collection in a Big Book or display format.

Possibilities for follow-up

- Read more haiku. Study the work of Basho, the exemplar of haiku poets. Discuss his work, comparing the poems to each other and picking out the familiar features in the work. Copy out and present a collection of these Japanese poems from the sixteenth century.
- Extend the writing of haiku into the writing of renga (a series of linked haiku); tanka (five lines in all, starting with five syllables in line one, then seven syllables in line two, five syllables in line three, and seven syllables each in lines four and five; and Ngu Utu (alternating lines of five and seven syllables in a poem of any length, ending with two rhymes of seven syllables).

Objectives

This workshop is relevant to many year groups, particularly for the following objectives.

Y3T2 Text 4, 5, 11: choose and prepare poems for performance; rehearse and improve performance; write new or extended verses for performance.

Y4T1 Text 14: write poems based on real/imagined experience.

Y4T2 Text 11: write poetry based on the structure/style of poems read.

Y4T3 Text 5, 6, 7, 14, 15: clap/count syllables; describe how poets use/do not use rhyme; recognise simple forms of poetry and their uses; experiment with writing different styles/structures; produce polished poetry through revision.

Kennings

Fin Flapper

Staring eyes
fair prize
golden darter
good gobbler
chase player
fast forgetter
flake eater
fin flapper.

Hill Hopper

Scratch scritcher
nose twitcher
thumb licker
bowl kicker
carrot cruncher
lettuce muncher
straw robber
tail bobber.

Guess what?

Round facer
no smiler
still stander
two hander
night friendly
heart beater
time keeper
sudden shrieker.

Michaela Morgan

© Michaela Morgan ISBN 1-85346-804-5

Fin Flapper

Key concepts

Kennings
Language choice and control
Creating new words.

Read! Speak! Listen! Enjoy!

- Photocopy and enlarge the poems so that the whole class can see them.
- Read the kenning aloud several times. Different readers read. Group reads.
- Readers try to guess the answer to the riddle 'Guess what?' (an alarm clock), 'Fin Flapper' (a goldfish), 'Hill Hopper' (a rabbit).
- Enjoy!

Discuss

- This kind of poem is called a kenning. Discuss the form of the poem.
- Kennings use a descriptive technique in which you avoid actually stating the name of the thing you are describing. Instead you use a compound, usually two-word, description of it; often you use a series of such descriptions. A historical example would be *sharp stabber* ('knife'). More current examples include *medicine man* ('doctor'), *ice box* ('fridge'), or *ankle-biter* ('baby')!
- Alliteration is commonly used in kennings.
- In Anglo-Saxon storytelling and verse you will find kennings. (See 'Possibilities for follow-up' below.)
- The length of the poems – kennings can be very short.
- The example poems rhyme, but kennings do not have to rhyme.

Analyse models

- How many words on a line?
- Other reasons behind the choice of words: the poet builds a mental picture of the thing he or she is describing, often leaving the most obvious clues till last. Thus a kenning can have elements of a riddle.

Write

- **Whole-class activity: write a kenning describing animals and everyday objects.**
  - Teacher as scribe.
  - Subjects might include: 'Tiger', 'Cat', 'Dog', 'Clock', 'Vacuum cleaner', 'Fridge', 'Pencil case'.
  - Think of the item you are describing and jot down the attributes attached to it.
  - Leave the most obvious ones (such as the stripes on a tiger) till last – or omit them.
  - Find two-word descriptions. So, instead of saying *fierce* and *hungry tiger*, write *fierce feeder*.
  - You can use alliteration and rhyme but these are not necessary.
- **Move on to independent work.** Pupils write a kenning, but leave out the last line (naming the subject) and see if the class can guess it.

Perform! Discuss! Enjoy! Applaud!

Plenary and revision/redrafting

- Read out and guess the subjects. Comment on particularly good choices of words.
- Make the point that poems are worked and reworked. Can anyone suggest improvements or alternatives?
- Incorporate revisions.
- Ask children to write or type out their lines – with revisions incorporated.
- Present as a collection in Big Book or display format.

Possibilities for follow-up

- Links can be made with riddles. See Appendix for an example of an Anglo-Saxon riddle. Invite pupils to guess the answer: probably ice.
- See also Appendix for an extract from *Beowulf*, an epic poem composed sometime between the eighth and the tenth century in the language known as Old English or Anglo-Saxon. Note the use of alliteration in both the extract and the riddle.
- Links can be made with list poems.

Objectives

This workshop is relevant to many year groups, particularly for the following objectives.

Y3T1 Text 7, 9, 12: distinguish between rhyming/non-rhyming poetry; generate ideas by brainstorming; collect suitable words/phrases for writing.

Y3T2 Text 4, 5: choose and prepare poems for performance; rehearse and improve performance.

Y3T3 Text 7: select/prepare/recite by heart poetry that plays with language.

Y4T1 Text 7, 14: compare/contrast poems on similar themes; write poems based on experience.

Y4T3 Text 15: produce polished poetry through revision.

Y5T2 Text 5, 6, 10, 12: perform poetry; understand poetic terms; literal/figurative language; write extensions using existing structures of poems.

Y6T2 Text 3, 5, 6, 8: recognise how poets manipulate words; analyse moods/feelings in poetry; interpret implied/multilayered meanings; analyse how writers evoke responses in readers.

Y6T3 Word 6, 7: practise/extend vocabulary; experiment with language.

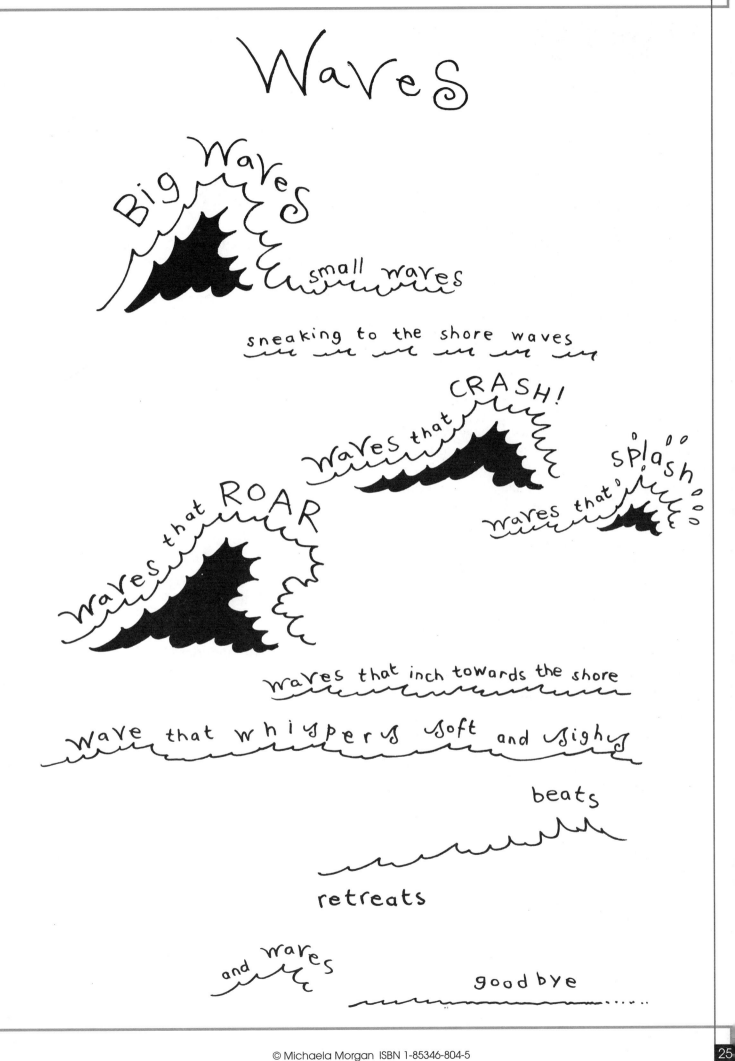

Waves

Big Waves

small waves

sneaking to the shore waves

Waves that CRASH!

Waves that ROAR

waves that SPLASH

waves that inch towards the shore

wave that whispers soft and sighs

beats

retreats

and waves

goodbye

Waves

Key concepts

Shape/concrete poetry
Wordplay
Calligrams.

Read! Speak! Listen! Enjoy!

- Photocopy and enlarge the poem so that the whole class can see it.
- Read the poem aloud several times. Different readers read – with expression, pace and volume appropriate to the words. Group reads.
- Look at the poem. It is in the shape of the thing it is describing.
- Enjoy!

Discuss

- This kind of poem is called a shape poem (or a concrete poem). The layout of the words represents the subject of the poem. A shape poem is always specially shaped to represent the subject, e.g. a shape poem about a banana will be banana-shaped.
- This poem also features calligrams. The formation of the letters – or the font used – represents the subject.
- This poem rhymes but a shape poem does not have to rhyme – most do not.

Analyse model

- Look at the language. Find examples of: onomatopoeia, alliteration, wordplay.
- Wordplay: in poetry one word may have more than one level of meaning. In this poem *beat* has several meanings ('to make a retreat', 'to defeat', 'to pound', 'to have a regular rhythmic movement or sound'). *Wave* also has more than one meaning – as a noun meaning 'a ridge of water that curls and breaks' and as a verb meaning 'to move one's hand to and fro in greeting'.
- Other reasons behind the choice of words: the poet builds a picture of the thing she is describing.

Write

- **Whole-class activity: write a shape poem.**
  - Teacher as scribe, taking suggestions from the class – modelling the process of brainstorming, note-jotting, choosing, changing, reading back, looking, listening, changing.
  - Subjects might include: a worm, a snake, rain, a spider's web, a hedgehog, an octopus, a flower.
  - First gather your thoughts about the subject. What would you want to say about a snake? How does it move? What sound does it make etc.? Brainstorm and gather words (*slither, slide, hiss, sneak...*). Use a dictionary, thesaurus and rhyming dictionary as appropriate. Think of words you can represent in shapes (*coil, twist, turn, loop...*). Then arrange your words in the shape of a snake or snakes.
  - Delete unnecessary words. Note that in the model poem, the poet does not says *Waves can be big, sometimes they roar...they splash all over* and so on.
  - Reorder the words for best effect.
  - You can use alliteration, onomatopoeia, similes, wordplay (*the snake snakes around*), etc.
  - Rhyme is an option but not a necessity.
- **Move on to independent work.** Pupils write shape poems using ideas of their own or from the whole-class session.

Perform! Discuss! Enjoy! Applaud!

Plenary and revision/redrafting

- Read out and show the poems. Comment on particularly good choices of words.
- Make the point that poems are worked and reworked. Can anyone suggest improvements or alternatives? Are there words that could be cut out? Descriptions that could be added?
- Incorporate revisions.
- Ask children to write or type out their lines – with revisions incorporated.
- Present as a collection in a Big Book or display format.

Possibilities for follow-up

Calligrams: collect synonyms and represent each word calligrammatically to convey the shades of meaning, e.g said, **BELLOWED**, *whispered*, *shrieeeeeekd*.

Objectives

This workshop is relevant to many year groups, particularly for the following objectives.

Y3T1 Text 7, 9, 12, 13: distinguish between rhyming/non-rhyming poetry; generate ideas through brainstorming; collect suitable words/phrases for writing; invent calligrams and shape poems.

Y3T3 Text 6, 15: compare forms/types of humour in poetry; write poetry using sound to create effects.

Y5T1 concrete poetry Word 7, 10: explain differences between synonyms; use adverbs in writing; Sentence 1: investigate word order and meaning; Text 7, 8, 16: analyse/compare poetic style; investigate/collect examples of wordplay; convey feelings/moods in a poem.

Y5T2 Word 11: onomatopoeia; Sentence 1, 3: reorder simple sentences; adapt writing for audiences and puposes; Text 12, 13: write extensions/additional verses for poems; review and edit for needs of readers.

Y5T3 Word 11: use dictionaries efficiently; Sentence 2: adapt writing for audiences/purposes.

Space Rap

(Chorus): Say oh oh (oh oh)
Say Solar System
Say oh oh (oh oh)
On a rappin' mission (on a rappin' mission).

Planet number one is Mercury
And this is known through all the galaxy.
It's hot, it's hot, like a steaming pot.
So close to the sun you'd toast like a bun
So living there would not be fun!

(Chorus)

The planet Venus is hotter still.
If you lived there you would be ill.
A place of gas and acid rain
Living there would be a pain!

(Chorus)

The planet Earth is number three.
The green is the land, the blue is the sea.
The average temperature is twenty-two.
We live here and that is true!

(Chorus)

Planet number four is the red one, Mars.
The name is famous – it's on chocolate bars.
It's a planet that has its own volcanoes.
It may have life there but nobody knows.

(Chorus)

Planet number five is Jupiter.
It's got a big hole, it'll make your mind stir.
It's the biggest planet of them all
Too big to use as – a football.

(Chorus)

Planet number six is called Saturn.
It orbits slowly but boy can it turn!
Saturn is a planet with icy rings
And in outer space it's one of the most colourful things.

(Chorus)

Planet number seven is Uranus.
If you landed there you would be famous.
It's minus two-hundred-and-ten degrees.
It's even got its very own seas.

(Chorus)

Neptune is planet eight.
It's always ready to rotate.
It's got a cloud by the name of Scooter.
It has a very nice blueish colour.

(Chorus)

Planet number nine is called Pluto.
It's made from ice and rock – so
the temperature is minus two-hundred-and-thirty degrees
Not like our planet – too cold for trees!

(Chorus)

Planet X is the unknown one.
As far as we know it's furthest from the sun.
Some think it's there. Some think it's not.
Until we know for sure, that's nine we've got.

(Chorus): Say oh oh (oh oh)
Say Solar System
Say oh oh (oh oh)
On a rappin' mission (on a rappin' mission).

By a group of children in a Leicestershire school,
based on 'Solar System' by Jimmy Grey

Space Rap

Key concepts

Performance poetry
Maintaining rhythm
Writing in rhyme.

Read! Speak! Listen! Enjoy!

- Photocopy and enlarge the poem so that the whole class can see it.
- Read the poem aloud several times with expression, pace, volume as appropriate. Different readers read. Group reads.
- Enjoy!

Discuss

- Who wrote this poem? (It is a collaborative poem. The class enjoyed a rap by Jimmy Grey from *Rap with Rosen*, published by Longman. All the class thought of a chorus and gathered ideas. Then groups chose a planet and wrote a stanza about that planet. They incorporated the information they had gathered in their study of the solar system.)
- Discuss subject matter, style, words used, form.
- Raps always rhyme and it's sometimes hard to find a rhyme. What can you do when this happens?
  - Rearrange the line so it ends with another word.
  - Choose another word to replace the one that is hard to rhyme with.
  - Use a rhyming dictionary.
- Sometimes poets make up words but they do this on purpose – it's easy when rhyming to be silly by accident!
- This rap has a chorus, which is quite simple but holds the whole poem together and is fun to join in with.

Analyse model

As this is a rap, it has an emphatic rhythm and rhyme scheme, and maintains a fast pace. Look at rhyme scheme in the model and beat out the rhythm. Are there any places where the rhythm needs tightening? Revise the poem and improve it where you can.

Write

- Whole-class activity: make up a chorus.
  - Take the topic you are currently working on and try to make up a refrain or chorus. Topic possibilities: 'Light', 'The Tudors', 'The Romans', 'Our School', 'Myself'.
  - Teacher as scribe.
  - Make up a chorus, e.g. for the Tudors:

    Divorced, beheaded, died
    Divorced, beheaded, survived.

  - Encourage the use of a dictionary, thesaurus and rhyming dictionary.
  - Groups or individuals write a stanza of the class-topic rap, e.g. for the Romans:

    We build roads straight and long
    We fought foes and won – we're strong...

- **Move on to independent work.**
  Pupils can write raps using ideas of their own or from the whole-class session.

Perform! Discuss! Enjoy! Applaud!

- Get together again and perform the chorus then listen to each stanza being performed. Applaud!
- Emphasise that these are drafts. Consider revisions. Are there any places where the rhythm or the rhyme could be improved? Scribe the whole piece working in revisions sensitively.
- Ask children to write or type out their lines – with revisions incorporated.
- Present as a collection in a Big Book or display format.

Possibilities for follow-up

- A public performance (assembly?) of the rap.
- Write the rap up for a display. Use lettering to stress volume and subject, e.g. *rap it BIG* and *rap it **bold***.
- Collect other raps to add to this display or anthology.
- Make a tape of the children rapping.
- Use percussion or other musical instruments to accompany.
- Rap your spelling lists!
- Ask groups to find another rap they like, perform it, and then explain what they like about that particular rap.
- Retell a legend, myth, or tale in a rap.

Objectives

This workshop is relevant to many year groups, particularly for the following objectives.

Y5T1 Text 7: consider impact of rhymes and other sound patterns.

Y5T2 Text 5, 6, 7, 11, 12: perform poems in variety of ways; understand terms describing types of poems; compile class anthology with commentaries; write own versions of myths/legends using specific structure; write extensions/additional verses for poems read.

Y5T3 choral and performance poetry from a variety of cultures Text 4, 5, 11: read/rehearse/modify poetry performance; select poetry for anthology and justify choices; use performance poems as models for writing – revise/redraft and present.

I am a Baggy Tee Shirt

I am a cheeky monkey, climbing and clambering.

I am a baggy tee shirt, hanging out.

I am a comfy sofa, relaxed, lounging.

I am the colour yellow, mellow and sunny.

I am a yellow pepper, fresh and cheerful.

I am a sunflower, waving in the sun.

I am a Rice Krispie, popping with fun!

By a group of children in an Essex school

I am a Baggy Tee Shirt

Read! Speak! Listen! Enjoy!

- Photocopy and enlarge the poem so that the whole class can see it.
- Read the poem aloud several times. Different readers read. Group reads.
- Enjoy!

Discuss

- Who wrote this poem?
- How old do you think the poem is?
- What clues can you find to the age of the poem? (Subject matter, style, words used, spellings, form.)
- A poem has carefully chosen words – sometimes the words are chosen to rhyme, sometimes they are chosen for their meaning, sometimes for their sound/music or alliteration. In this case, apart from the final two lines, the words do not rhyme. Instead, what is special is the use of figurative language to conjure up mental pictures.
- Through the language in the poem we gain a picture of the person described. Are they tall or short? Tense or relaxed? Friendly? Fun? Serious? Dark? Blonde?
- The poem uses metaphor. When a writer uses a metaphor he or she makes a comparison but does not say one thing is like another. He or she says one thing is another, e.g. *She is pure poison.*

Analyse model

- Can you find any alliteration?
- Find the only example of a rhyme in the poem. Discuss the effectiveness of ending the poem with a rhyming couplet.

✍ Write

- **Whole-class activity: write a description of a well-known character.**
  - Teacher as scribe, demonstrating the process of writing, thinking, crossing out and improving.
  - Subjects might include: a character in fiction, or a pop or film star.
  - Describe the person as some of the following: an animal, bird, or fish; a plant or flower; an item of furniture; a vehicle; a colour; a food or drink; an item of clothing; a building.
  - Try to end the poem on a rhyming couplet.
- **Move on to independent work.** Pupils write poems describing themselves, their friends, or 'mystery' characters.

Perform! Discuss! Enjoy! Applaud!

Plenary and revision/redrafting

- Read out and comment on particularly good choices of words. In the case of 'mystery' poems, guess who has been described.
- Remind the children of the definition of a metaphor. Which metaphors have they particularly enjoyed – why?
- Make the point that poems are worked and reworked. Can anyone suggest improvements or alternatives?
- Incorporate revisions.
- Ask children to write or type out their lines – with revisions incorporated.
- Present as a collection in Big Book or display format.

Possibilities for follow-up

Take *one* of the metaphors used in the whole-class poem and develop it.

The Sound Collector

A stranger called this morning
Dressed all in black and grey
Put every sound into a bag
And carried them away

The whistling of the kettle
The turning of the lock
The purring of the kitten
The ticking of the clock

The popping of the toaster
The crunching of the flakes
When you spread the marmalade
The scraping noise it makes

The hissing of the frying-pan
The ticking of the grill
The bubbling of the bathtub
As it starts to fill

The drumming of the raindrops
On the window pane
When you do the washing up
The gurgle of the drain

The crying of the baby
The squeaking of the chair
The swishing of the curtain
The creaking of the stair

A stranger called this morning
He didn't leave his name
Left us only silence
Life will never be the same.

Roger McGough

The Sound Collector

Key concepts

Onomatopoeia
Following a rhyme scheme.

Read! Speak! Listen! Enjoy!

- Photocopy and enlarge the poem so that the whole class can see it.
- Read the poem aloud several times. Different readers read. Group reads.
- Enjoy!

Discuss

- Who wrote this poem?
- How old do you think the poem is?
- What clues can you find to the age of the poem? (Subject matter, style, words used, form.)
- Onomatopoeia – words which demonstrate the sounds they are describing – is a feature of this poem (e.g. *whistling, popping*). How many examples of onomatopoeia can you find in the poem?

Analyse model

- Discuss the form of the poem. How many lines to a stanza? Does it rhyme? (Quatrains with second and fourth lines rhyming; the rhyme scheme is *abcb*.)
- A poem has carefully chosen words – sometimes the words are chosen to rhyme, sometimes they are chosen for their meaning, sometimes for their sound/music or alliteration. In this case, they have been chosen for their rhyme, rhythm and onomatopoeia.
- The poem tells a story. It is a narrative poem. The four-line stanza is the form used for traditional narrative poems – ballads.
- How would you describe the mood of this poem?

✎ Write

- **Whole-class activity: add further stanzas to the poem.**
  - Can you suggest words to describe each sound, e.g. *glug* for *gurgle*. Write them on the model.
  - Read the poem again with some readers making the sounds (*hiss, pop, glug*) after the appropriate line.

- Teacher as scribe.
- Add further stanzas. Subjects might include: the telly, a sister on the phone, a mother's moan, a humming fridge, a whining brother, a grumbling gran, a computer game, a pet. (Some pupils will benefit from doing this as a group or individual activity.)
- **Move on to independent work.**
  - Pupils write a poem, or a stanza of a poem, based on the model, but with the stranger stealing the noises from the school or playground. You can use the writing frame at the end of this workshop to help – but feel free to modify the model if you need to.
  - First think of the sounds of school (clock *ticking*, pencils *scritch-scratching*, paint *sploshing*, *shrieking* from the playground, *thumping* from the hall, *clattering* of cutlery...) Use a thesaurus, dictionary and rhyming dictionary as appropriate.
  - Words to help: *squeaking, creaking, scratching, door, floor, chalk, talk, pattering, sploshing, dripping, taps, hamster, dropping, books, turning, pages, shushing, bell, ringing, singing, in the hall, hushing, screaming, from the playground, piercing, whistle, shriek, squeaking, new shoes, drawer, quiet, creak, scratching, pencil, sudden, splosh, paint, birds, outside.*

Perform! Discuss! Enjoy! Applaud!

Plenary and revision/redrafting

- Read out and comment on particularly good choices of words.
- Make the point that poems are worked and reworked. Can anyone suggest improvements or alternatives?
- Incorporate revisions.
- Ask children to write or type out their lines – with revisions incorporated.
- Present as a collection in a Big Book or display format.

Possibilities for follow-up

- Read other poems by Roger McGough.
- Collect examples of onomatopoeia from everyday language.
- Invent examples. For example, make up new onomatopoeic words to describe manufactured products (a new cleaning liquid, glue, sweets, drinks, foods, etc.).
- Look at traditional ballads and other narrative poems. Read these aloud. Discuss and compare them.

Objectives

This workshop is relevant to many year groups, particularly for the following objectives.

Y3T3 Text 15: onomatopoeia.

Y4T1 Text 8: find out more about popular authors.

Y4T2 Text 7, 11: identify patterns of rhyme and verse; write poetry based on structure/style of poems read.

Y4T3 Text 4, 5, 6, 7, 9, 15: understand/identify poetic terms; clap/count syllables; describe how poet uses/does not use rhyme; recognise simple forms of poetry and their uses; read further poems by favourite author; produce polished poetry through revision.

Y5T1 Text 6: read a number of poems by significant poets.

Y5T2 Word 11: onomatopoeia; Text 4, 5, 6, 7, 12: read a range of narrative poems; perform poems in a variety of ways; understand terms describing types of poems; compile class anthology of favourite poems; write extensions/additional verses for poems read.

Y5T3 Text 4, 11: rehearse/modify performance of poetry; use performance poems as models for writing – revise, redraft, and present.

Y6T1 Word 9: understand how new words are added to the language.

Y6T2 Text 3, 4, 9: recognise how poets manipulate words; investigate humorous verse; significant poets and their work.

Y6T3 Word 7: experiment with language; Text 3, 5, 6: describe/evaluate poet's style; compare/contrast work of one writer; connections/contrasts in work of different writers.

Writing frame

The School Sound Collector

A stranger called this morning

Dressed all in black and grey

Put every sound into a bag

And carried them away

The _____ of the _____ (a)

The _____ of the _____ (b rhyme here)

The _____ of the _____ (c)

The _____ of the _____ (b rhyme here)

The _____ of the _____

The _____ of the _____ (rhyme here)

The _____ of the _____

The _____ of the _____ (rhyme here)

A stranger called this morning

He didn't leave his name

Left us only silence

Life will never be the same.

Nocturnophobia

I am scared of the dark

Like a tree is nervous of Autumn

Like a pencil is terrified of an eraser

Like a window is anxious about a football

Like a log is horrified by a chainsaw

Like a car is afraid of the crusher

I am scared of the dark.

By a group of children in an East Sussex school

Nocturnophobia

Key concepts

Personification
Free verse
Similes
Invented language.

Read! Speak! Listen! Enjoy!

- Photocopy and enlarge the poem so that all the class can see it.
- Read the poem aloud several times. Different readers read. Group reads.
- Enjoy!

Discuss

- Who wrote this poem? (It is a collaborative poem – with many children contributing a line to it.)
- The lack of rhyme. A poem has carefully chosen words – sometimes the words are chosen to rhyme, sometimes they are chosen for their meaning, sometimes for their sound/music or alliteration. In this case, the words have been chosen for their images – for their figurative language. The poem is in free verse. It has no rhymes but the language is still carefully chosen.
- The children have invented a word for their title. *Nocturne* is a reference to night and *phobia* is fear, so their title means 'fear of the night'. Poets sometimes invent new words or portmanteau terms – joining two words together to make a new word. There are many examples of this in Lewis Carroll's 'Jabberwocky'.

Analyse model

- Look at the form of this poem. It starts with the poets telling us something about themselves (*I am scared of the dark*).This is autobiographical detail.
- Then there are a number of comparisons made. These are similes – one thing is described as being like another. The similes help us to understand more fully what is being described. The feeling of being scared is described and the imagery used helps us to understand that feeling by putting the feeling into word pictures.

- At the end of the list of similes the poets repeat their first line.
- The poem is in free verse. It is not limited by rhyme or rhythm, although there is a rhythm and pattern to it.
- The things being described are inanimate objects (a tree, a log, a car) not people. But they are described as if they are people – with the feelings of people. The poets have used personification.

✎ Write

- **Whole-class activity: write a poem based on the model.**
  - Teacher as scribe.
  - Start with *I am scared of . . .* Discuss and list synonyms for scared of *(terrified of/by, petrified of/by, nervous of, worried by, fearful of,* etc.). Encourage the use of a dictionary and thesaurus.
  - Continue the poem using similes and personification as in the model.
  - You can write other group poems varying the subject matter (*I am happy about...; I look forward to...; I am hopeful about...; I am fed up with...*).
- **Move on to independent work.**
  - Individual children can write their own poems. These poems can be connected into a sequence of poems describing feelings.
  - Pupils can make up their own titles. They can invent a word as the poets of the model poem did. Use an etymological dictionary to help.

Perform! Discuss! Enjoy! Applaud!

Plenary and revision/redrafting

- Read out and comment on particularly good choices of words.
- Make the point that poems are worked and reworked. Can anyone suggest improvements or alternatives?
- Incorporate revisions.
- Ask children to write or type out their lines – with revisions incorporated.
- Present as a sequence on feelings. These poems are linked by their theme and form.
- Make a book or display.

Possibilities for follow-up

Collect and read other poems about fears and feelings.

Objectives

This workshop is relevant to many year groups, particularly for the following objectives.

Y6T1 Text 10: write poems experimenting with active verbs and personification – revise.

Y6T2 Text 5: analyse how messages, moods, feelings, and attitudes are conveyed in poetry.

Y6T3 Word 7: experiment with language/create new words, similes, and metaphors; Text 2, 4, 13: discuss how linked poems relate to one another by theme/format/repetition; comment critically on the overall impact of a poem; write sequence of poems linked by theme or form.

Three

I met a miniature King
by the side of the road,
wearing a crown
and an ermine suit –
important, small,
plump as a natterjack toad,
Kneel! he shrieked, *Kneel for the King!*
CERTAINLY not, I said, *I'll do no such thing.*

I saw a Giantess,
tall as a tree.
You'll do for a new doll, she bellowed,
just the toy for me!
Into the box! Scream hard! Scream long!
I stared at her mad, pond eyes
then skipped away.
Dream on . . .

I bumped into Invisible Boy – *ouch!* –
at the edge of the field.
Give me a chocolate drop
said a voice.
What do you say?
Please.
So I did
then stared as it floated mid-air
and melted away.
These are three of the people I met yesterday.

Carol Ann Duffy

Three

Key concepts

Levels of meaning
Idioms and wordplay
Link with fable and myth

Redrafting
Figurative language
Half-rhyme.

Read! Speak! Listen! Enjoy!

- Photocopy and enlarge the poem so that the whole class can see it.
- Read the poem aloud several times. Different readers read with appropriate expression, pace and volume. Group reads.
- Enjoy!

Discuss

- Who wrote this poem?
- How old do you think the poem is?
- What clues can you find to the age of the poem? (Subject matter, style, words used, spellings, form.)
- Rhyme. A poem has carefully chosen words – sometimes the words are chosen to rhyme, sometimes they are chosen for their meaning, sometimes for their sound/music or alliteration. This poem has an irregular use of rhyme. Find the rhymes.
- The poem also has an uneven number of lines. it combines free verse with the occasional rhyme. It is a contemporary poem – contemporary poems are often looser than traditional ones.

Analyse model

- This poem has a dreamlike, fantasy feel to it. Each stanza starts with the narrator meeting a figure from a fantasy/myth/fairy tale. The poem illustrates the benefits of using your previous reading, experience and dreams when reading and writing.
- Language. Find alliteration. Find rhymes, including assonance and half rhymes (*Scream long!* and *Dream on...*) and internal rhymes (*stared... mid-air*). Find synonyms for *said*.
- Discuss the description of the king. Pick out the descriptions you like.
  - Comment on the juxtaposition of *important* and *small* – is this unexpected? Contradictory? What impression does it give of him?

- Comment on the word *plump*. What other synonyms for *plump* can you suggest? What effect does each word have?
- Discuss the comparison of the king with a toad. Point out that this is a simile – does it work?
- Look at the description of the eyes of the Giantess (*mad, pond eyes*). What does this description mean? Point out that this is a metaphor – her eyes are described as if they really are ponds. Think of what a pond is like (murky, perhaps deep, without reflection).
- Idioms. Comment on *I bumped into...* Point out that this is an idiomatic expression, but that here the poet has played with the words using the idiom as if was literally true (*I bumped into Invisible Boy – ouch*). The poet has also played with the cliché *Dream on...* Here it has two meanings ('No, I won't!' and 'I will carry on with my dreamy journey'). Poems often use wordplay. Think of other idiomatic expressions that you could play with by using them literally (e.g *He laughed his head off; I kept an eye on my little sister; She asked me to lend a hand.*)
- Look at the line breaks. Why has the poet chosen to end the lines where she has?
  - In the third stanza, why is *So I did* on a line all by itself? (It gives the line emphasis and pause. Line breaks tell us how to read the poem and pace our reading.)
  - In the first stanza, look at *Kneel! he shrieked, Kneel for the King!* – all on one line for a faster pace. The same applies to *Into the box! Scream hard! Scream long!* Keeping this all on one line makes for a quicker pace – a hint of frenzy.
  - Note that the poet does not always use full sentences. She uses an economical style. Discuss how *just the toy for me! Into the box!* is more dramatic than *You are just the toy for me. Get into this box.*). Point out the economy of poetry – how poets cut out unnecessary words. Find other examples of this (*I saw a Giantess, tall as a tree.* not *I saw a Giantess. She was as tall as a tree.*)
- Look at the punctuation in the poem. Note the clues it gives us about the tone, mood, pace.

✍ Write

- **Whole-class activity: using a writing frame.**
  - Complete the writing frame at the end of the workshop.

– Teacher as scribe, modelling the process of choosing words, changing one's mind, revising, cutting out unecessary words, using rhymes or alliteration, making a comparison, etc.

- **Move on to independent work.** Pupils write their own stanza. Creatures met could be: a dragon, a knight, a hero, an angel, a witch or a monster.

Perform! Discuss! Enjoy! Applaud!

Plenary and revision/redrafting

- Read out and comment on particularly good choices of words, punctuation, line breaks, wordplay, comparisons, etc.
- Make the point that poems are worked and reworked. Can anyone suggest improvements or alternatives? Discuss improvements made and the effects they had.
- Incorporate revisions.
- Ask children to write or type out their lines – with revisions incorporated.
- Present as a collection in Big Book or display format.

Possibilities for follow-up

- Link the children's individual poems to make a series poem for performance.
- Turn the poem into a play script and perform.
- Link with work on fable and myth.
- Link with work on idioms. See Appendix: 'Figuratively Speaking'.

Objectives

This workshop is relevant to many year groups, particularly for the following objectives.

Y5T1 Word 7, 9: synonyms; idiomatic phrases/clichés; Sentence 3, 6: discuss/edit/proofread own writing; puncutation as an aid to reader; Text 4, 6, 7, 8: consider how texts can be rooted in writer's experience; read a number of poems by significant poets; analyse forms/styles/themes of significant poets; investigate/collect examples of wordplay.

Y5T2 Word 12: metaphorical expressions/figures of speech; Text 1, 5, 10, 11, 12, 13: identify/classify feature of myths/legends/fables; perform poems in variety of ways; literal/figurative language; write own versions of myths/fables using specific structures; write extensions/additional verses for poems read; review/edit writing for identified readers.

Y5T3 Text 4,5: read/rehearse/modify performance; select poetry and justify choices.

Writing frame

One

I met a (*who/what did you meet? – someone/thing from a legend/myth/fairy tale*)

(*where did you meet him/her/it?*)_____

(*describe him/her/it*) _____

_____

(*what did he/she/it say?*) _____

_____

(*what did you say/do?*) _____

_____

This is one of the people I met yesterday.

Now check this over.
Cut out unnecessary words.
Put in strong, carefully chosen words.
Check that your punctuation will give your reader clues as to how to read this – where to pause, exclaim, etc.
Look at your line breaks.
Are there any changes you can make to improve your poem?

December

De snow, de sleet, de lack of heat,
De wishy-washy sunlight,
De lip turn blue, de cold, "ACHOO!"
De runny nose, de frostbite

De creakin' knee, de misery
De joint dem all rheumatic,
De icy bed, (de blanket dead)
De burs' pipe in de attic

De window a-shake, de glass near break,
De wind dat cut like razor
De wonderin' why you never buy
De window from dat double-glazer

De thick new coat, zip up to the throat,
De nose an' ears all pinky,
De weepin' sky, de clothes can't dry,
De days dem long an' inky.

De icy road, de heavy load,
De las' minute Christmas shoppin'
De cuss an' fret 'cause you feget
De ribbon an' de wrappin'.

De mud, de grime, de slush, de slime,
De place gloomy since November,
De sinkin' heart, is jus' de start, o'
De wintertime,
December.

Valerie Bloom

December

Key concepts

Poems reflecting different cultures and voices
Internal rhyme
Comparison of different treatment of classic and contemporary themes.

Read! Speak! Listen! Enjoy!

- Photocopy and enlarge the poem so that the whole class can see it.
- Read the poem aloud several times. Different readers read. Group reads.
- Enjoy!

Discuss

- Who wrote this poem?
- How old do you think the poem is? What clues can you find to its age? (Subject matter, style, words used, spellings, form.)
- Notice that the poet has used the voice, rhythm and accent of the Caribbean. Pick out examples of these.
- Form, rhyme and rhythm.
  - A poem has carefully chosen words – sometimes the words are chosen to rhyme, sometimes they are chosen for their meaning, sometimes for their sound/music or alliteration. This poem is in quatrains and has a lively rhythm. The pace is emphasised by the rhyme.
  - On lines 1 and 3 in each stanza there are rhymes within the lines (internal rhymes). These increase the pace of the poem. Look at the last stanza. How does the poet slow the poem down to finish it?

Analyse model

- How does the poet make this poem sound so real and contemporary?
- Pick out and discuss particular lines and words you like. What gives them their appeal?
- Who do you think is speaking in this poem? Do the concerns with cold, rheumatism, etc. hint at a certain age? How would the poem differ if written from a child's perspective? If written by an Australian?

✎ Write

- **Whole-class activity: using a writing frame.**
  - Teacher as scribe, modelling the process of gathering thoughts, changing one's mind, searching for words, redrafting, etc.
  - Complete the writing frame at the end of the workshop. Valerie Bloom has written about the unpleasantness of December. Think about the good things associated with December and complete the frame accordingly.
- **Move on to independent work.** Pupils write their own stanza about December. You could also try March, May or November.

Perform! Discuss! Enjoy! Applaud!

Plenary and revision/redrafting

- Read out and comment on particularly good choices of words.
- Make the point that poems are worked and reworked. Can anyone suggest improvements or alternatives?
- Incorporate revisions.
- Ask children to write or type out their lines – with revisions incorporated.
- Present as a collection in Big Book or display format.

Possibilities for follow-up

- Read other poems about the seasons. Compile an anthology of poems on this subject.

- Valerie Bloom's poem has been modelled on a well-known poem by Thomas Hood. (See Appendix: 'November'). Enlarge Hood's poem and compare the two. Go through the discussion and analysis points with Hood's poem. Explain that Novembers were foggier in Thomas Hood's time! Both poems use a particular voice capturing a particular time and culture. Both employ informal language.

- Practise performing 'November' by Thomas Hood and 'December' by Valerie Bloom. Then put together stanzas made by children to form a class poem to perform.

- Groups or individuals can take a month of the year and write a stanza about it. This can be put together to make the 'Poem of the Year'. Each month can be in a separate form and style, revisiting different styles of poetry encountered by the children, e.g. kennings, use of metaphor, use of personification, etc.

Objectives

This workshop is relevant to many year groups, particularly for the following objectives.

Y5T1 Text 7, 12, 16: analyse and compare style/forms/themes of significant poets; discuss appeal of established/'classic' authors; convey feelings/moods in poems.

Y5T2 longer classic poetry Text 5, 6, 7, 12: perform poems in variety of ways; understand terms describing types of poems; compile class anthology with commentaries; write extensions/additional verses for poems read.

Y5T3 poems from a variety of cultures and traditions, choral and performance poetry Word 9: transform words (negation/comparison); Text 1, 2, 3, 4, 5, 6, 9: investigate texts from different cultures; indentify/change point of view; read/rehearse/modify performance; select poetry and justify choices; explore older literature; write in the style of the author.

Y6T1 Word 7, 9: understand how words/expression change meaning over time; understand how new words are added to the language; Text 2, 3, 4, 5: take account of viewpoint; articulate personal responses to literature; be familiar with work of some established authors; contribute constructively to shared discussion about literature.

Y6T2 Word 7: use known spellings as basis for spelling new words. Text 3, 4, 5, 9: recognise how poets manipulate words; investigate humorous verse; analyse moods/feelings in poetry; increase familiarity with significant poets of past.

Y6T3 Word 7: experiment with language/create words, similes, and metaphors; Text 2, 3, 4, 6, 13: describe/evaluate style of individual poet; discuss linked poems according to theme/format/repetition; comment critically on overall impact of poem; look at connections/contrasts in work of different writers; write sequence of poems linked by theme/form.

Writing frame

December

De eyes a glow, the skies of _____

De shall we have a snow fight?

De toasty feet, the fire's _____

De starshine and de moon _____

De frost all round, de slidey_____

De Christmas tills a'ringin'

De seasonal sights, de twinkly _____

De Christmas songs for_____

Hubble Bubble

From Macbeth

Thrice the brinded cat hath mew'd
Thrice, and once the hedge-pig whin'd.
Harpier cries: 'tis time, 'tis time.

Round about the cauldron go;
In the poison'd entrails throw.
Toad, that under cold stone
Days and nights has thirty-one
Swelter'd venom, sleeping got,
Boil thou first in the charmed pot.

Double, double toil and trouble:
Fire, burn; and, cauldron, bubble.

Fillet of a fenny snake,
In the cauldron boil and bake;
Eye of newt, and toe of frog,
Wool of bat, and tongue of dog,
Adder's fork, and blind-worm's sting,
Lizard's leg, and howlet's wing,
For a charm of powerful trouble,
Like a hell-broth boil and bubble.
Double, double toil and trouble
Fire, burn; and, cauldron, bubble.

William Shakespeare

Dinner on Elm Street

Thrice the old school cat hath spewed.
Teachers shriek and children whine:
Ring the bell! 'Tis time! 'Tis time!

Round about the cauldron go,
In the mouldy cabbage throw,
Stone-cold custard, thick with lumps,
Germs from Kevin (sick with mumps).
Boil up sprouts for the greenish smell,
add sweaty sock, cheese pie as well.

Froth and splutter, boil and bubble.
March them in here at the double.

Fillet of an ancient steak
In the cauldron boil and bake.
Eye of spud and spawn of frog,
A chocolate moose, a heated dog.
Add the goo from 'twixt the toes
And crusty bits from round the nose.

Froth and splutter, boil and bubble.
March them in here at the double.

Lumpy mincemeat, grey and gristly,
Giblets, gizzards, all things grizzly.
Beak of chicken in a nugget,
with greasy chips the kids will love it.
Scab of knee sprinkle in,
squeeze juice of pimple from a chin.
Here's the spell 'twill make you thinner.
It's the nightmare Elm Street dinner.

Froth and splutter, boil and bubble.
March them in here at the double!

Michaela Morgan

© Michaela Morgan ISBN 1-85346-804-5

Hubble Bubble

Key concepts

Comparison of different treatment of classic and contemporary themes
Using existing poems to write extensions based on these
Familiarity with classic authors.

Read! Speak! Listen! Enjoy!

- Photocopy and enlarge the poems so that the whole class can see them. Read them aloud.
- Group reads refrain.
- Enjoy!

Discuss

- Who wrote these poems?
- How old do you think the poems are? What clues can you find to their age? (Name of poet, subject matter, style, words used, form.)

Analyse model

- Read the poem modelled on the Shakespeare. What similarities can you find? (Similar words, rhythm, rhyme scheme, use of refrain, mood.)
- Both poems have a strong rhyme and rhythm. Find the rhymes and beat out the rhythm. Both have refrains. Find and compare these.

✍ Write

- **Whole-class activity: write a spell using a writing frame.**
  - Make up refrains. For example:

    Stir and chop, stir and chop
    Add it to the cooking pot.
    Boil and steam, boil and steam
    Here's a spell to make you scream.

  - Teacher as scribe.
  - Attempt to complete the writing frame at the end of the workshop.
  - List possible ingredients and encourage the addition of adjectives.
  - Spot opportunities for rhyme and alliteration.
  - Encourage the use of a thesaurus or cookery book (to find suitable culinary terms, e.g. *stir in, blend, chop, heat, eat, slice, grate, grind, bake, bind, mix, make, sprinkle, bake, roast, toast, fry,* etc.).
  - Encourage the use of a rhyming dictionary.

- **Move on to independent work.**
  - Pupils to write spells with or without the writing frame. Even when using the frame, some modifications to the frame should be allowed. The frame is a support not a straitjacket! It should provide a starting point.
  - Possible subjects for spells:
    'A Spell to Make a Perfect Poem' (ingredients: rhythm, rhyme, etc.)
    'A Spell to Make an Adventure/Mystery/Science-Fiction Story' (following discussion of genres of fiction)
    'A Spell to Pollute the Planet'
    'A Spell to Save the Planet'
    'A Spell to Make a Perfect Friend'.

Perform! Discuss! Enjoy! Applaud!

Plenary and revision/redrafting

- Read out and comment on particularly good choices of words.
- Make the point that poems are worked and reworked. Can anyone suggest improvements or alternatives?
- Points to consider: maintaining a rhythm; deleting or adding words; using strong adjectives; reordering words and lines for better effect; using a variety of synonyms – culinary terms – as well as *add*; using punctuation.
- Incorporate revisions.
- Ask children to write or type out their lines – with revisions incorporated.
- Present as a collection in Big Book or display format.

Possibilities for follow-up

Instead of writing a spell, write a recipe (see Appendix: 'Recipe for a Story'). This is less challenging, as it does not require a grasp of the rhyme and rhythm scheme.

Objectives

This workshop is relevant to many year groups, particularly for the following objectives.

Y5T1 Word 7: synonyms; Sentence 1, 3: investigate word order; discuss/proofread/edit own writing.

Y5T2 Word 9: collect/define/spell technical words from other subjects; Sentence 1: reorder simple sentences; Text 5, 12: perform poems in variety of ways; write extensions/additional verses for poems read.

Y5T3 Word 11: use a range of dictionaries effectively; Text 4, 6, 9, 11: read/rehearse/perform poetry; explore older literature; write in the style of the author; use performance poems as models for writing – revise/redraft/present.

Y6T1 Word 7: understand how words/expressions change meaning over time. Sentence 6: secure knowledge of sophisticated punctuation; Text 3, 4, 5, 6: articulate personal responses to literature; be familiar with work of established authors; contribute constructively to shared discussion about literature; manipulate narrative perspective (write in voice/style of a text; produce modern retelling).

Y6T2 Text 3, 9, 10: recognise how poets manipulate words; increase familiarity with significant writers of past; use different genres as writing models.

Y6T3 Text 6: connections/contrasts in work of different writers.

Writing frame

Spell

Round about the _____ go:

In the _____ throw.

_____

_____

_____

Boil thou first in the charmed pot.

(Refrain): _____

_____

_____

In the cauldron boil and_____

_____

_____

_____

For a charm of powerful trouble,

Like a hell broth boil and bubble.

(Refrain): _____

_____

The Dead Quire

I

Beside the Mead of Memories,
Where Church-way mounts to
    Moaning Hill,
The sad man sighed his
    phantasies –
He seems to sigh them still.

II

"'Twas the Birth-tide Eve, and the
    hamleteers
Made merry with ancient
    Mellstock zest,
But the Mellstock quire of former
    years
Had entered into rest.

III

"Old Dewy lay by the gaunt yew
    tree,
And Reuben and Michael a pace
    behind,
And Bowman with his family
By the wall that the ivies bind.

IV

"The singers had followed one by
    one,
Treble, and tenor, and thorough-
    bass;
And the worm that wasteth had
    begun
To mine their mouldering place.

V

"For two-score years, ere Christ-
    day light,
Mellstock had throbbed to strains
    from these:
But now there echoed on the
    night
No Christmas harmonies.

VI

"Three meadows off, at a
    dormered inn,
The youth had gathered in high
    carouse,
And, ranged on settles, some
    therein
Had drunk them to a drowse.

VII

"Loud, lively, reckless, some had
    grown,
Each dandling on his jigging knee
Eliza, Dolly, Nance, or Joan –
Livers in levity.

VIII

"The taper flames and hearthfire
    shine
Grew smoke-hazed to a lurid light,
And songs on subjects not divine
Were warbled forth that night.

IX

"Yet many were sons and
    grandsons here
Of those who, on such eves gone
    by,
At that still hour had throated
    clear
Their anthems to the sky.

X

"The clock belled midnight; and
    ere long
One shouted, 'Now 'tis Christmas
    morn;
Here's to our women old and
    young,
And to John Barleycorn!'

XI

"They drink the toast and shout
    again;
The pewter-ware rings back the
    boom,
And for a breath-while follows
    then
A silence in the room.

XII

"When nigh without, as in old
    days,
The ancient quire of voice and
    string
Seemed singing words of prayer
    and praise
As they had used to sing:

XIII

"*While shepherds watch'd their
    flocks by night, –*
Thus swells the long familiar sound
In many a quaint symphonic
    flight –
To, *Glory shone around.*

XIV

"The sons defined their fathers'
    tones,
The widow his whom she had
    wed,
And others in the minor moans
The viols of the dead.

XV

"Something supernal has the
    sound
As verse by verse the strain
    proceeds,
And stilly staring on the gound
Each roysterer holds and heeds.

XVI

"Towards its chorded closing bar
Plaintively, thinly, waned the hymn,
Yet lingered, like the notes afar
Of banded seraphim.

XVII

"With brows abashed, and
    reverent tread,
The hearkeners sought the tavern
    door:
But nothing, save wan moonlight,
    spread
The empty highway o'er.

XVIII
"While on their bearing fixed and
    tense
The aerial music seemed to sink,
As it were gently moving thence
Along the river brink.

XIX
"Then did the Quick pursue the
    Dead
By crystal Froom that crinkles
    there;
And still the viewless quire ahead
Voiced the old holy air.

XX
"By Bank-walk wicket, brightly
    bleached,
It passed, and 'twixt the hedges
    twain,
Dogged by the living; till it
    reached
The bottom of Church Lane.

XXI
"There at the turning, it was heard
Drawing to where the churchyard
    lay:
But when they followed
    thitherward
It smalled, and died away.

XXII
"Each gravestone of the quire,
    each mound,
Confronted them beneath the
    moon;
But no more floated therearound
That ancient Birth-night tune.

XXIII
"There Dewy lay by the gaunt
    yew tree,
There Reuben and Michael, a
    pace behind,
And Bowman with his family
By the wall that the ivies bind . . .

XXIV
"As from a dream each sobered
    son
Awoke, and musing reached his
    door;
'Twas said that of them all, not
    one
Sat in a tavern more."

XXV
– The sad man ceased; and
    ceased to heed
His listener, and crossed the leaze
From Moaning Hill towards the
    mead –
The Mead of Memories.

Thomas Hardy

The Dead Quire

Key concepts

Classic narrative poetry
Ballad
Language change over time
In-depth discussion and analysis of poem.

Read! Speak! Listen! Enjoy!

- Photocopy and enlarge the poem so that the whole class can see it.
- Read the poem aloud with appropriate expression.
- This is a longer narrative poem – a classic. Explain to the children that there may be unfamiliar words and it may not be completely clear on first reading – but they can just listen and enjoy the sound, the mood, and general impression.
- Enjoy!

Discuss

- Who wrote this poem?
- How old do you think the poem is? (Thomas Hardy lived from 1840 to 1928 but this poem seems even older. The poet has given it an antique feel by using a traditional form and subject matter, and archaic vocabulary (*'Twas, ere, nigh*, etc.).
- What clues can you find to the age of this poem? (Subject matter, form, style, words used, spellings. Point out that meanings of words and spellings of words have changed over time. Look for examples of these in the poem and demonstrate the contemporary spelling.)
- The length of the poem – poems can be very short or very long. This is a narrative poem, which means that it tells a story. This type of poem is often long.
- Rhyme. A poem has carefully chosen words – sometimes the words are chosen to rhyme, sometimes they are chosen for their meaning, sometimes for their sound/music or alliteration. Discuss the rhyme scheme in this poem. (It goes *abab*.)
- Each stanza is a quatrain, having four lines. This is the traditional form of the ballad – an antique storytelling poem.

Analyse model

Select and focus on some of these aspects – too extensive and intensive a study risks deadening the poem. You can return to the poem from time to time to make further points.

- What is the plot of this poem? Attempt to extract and retell the story. Considering the following questions will aid comprehension.
  – Who is telling this tale? (See stanzas I and XXV.)
  – What time of year is it? (See stanza II.)
  – Where is the choir? (See stanzas III and IV.)
  – What are the names of the members of the choir? (See stanza III.)
  – How long have they been dead? (See stanza V.)
  – What are the young villagers doing? (See stanzas VI, VII, and VIII.)
  – What happens in stanzas XII to XVI?
  – In XIX the live revellers run after the ghostly choir. What is the name of the river they run beside?
  – XXIII is a repeated stanza. (See stanza III.) Discuss repetition – why do you think the poet repeats himself? Is this a mistake or intentional?
  – Discuss the final stanza. Is it an effective ending? Does it repeat a previous stanza? Discuss the importance of endings and beginnings. Point out the circularity of some tales – how ending where you began can be a satisfying conclusion to a story or a poem.
- Vocabulary.
  – Some of the vocabulary in this poem will be strange to contemporary children. Guess the meaning of some of the vocabulary, e.g. *Birth-tide Eve, Christ-day light, hearthfire shrine, throated, clock belled midnight, John Barleycorn, a breath-while, stilly, the Quick...the Dead, smalled.*
  – Physically demonstrate some of the vocabulary, for example ask children to move as described in stanza *XVII with brows abashed and reverent tread.*
  – Ask the children to be Dictionary Detectives. Give groups of children particular words to look up, then ask them to report back to the class explaining any unfamiliar language. Some of the words to investigate are: *Mead, phantasies* (note how the spelling has changed

over time), *hamleteers* (look up *hamlet*), *zest, gaunt, two-score* (look up *score*), *carouse, levity, taper, warbled, anthems, viols.*

- Find examples of alliteration.
- Find examples of compound descriptions (as in kennings), for example *a breath-while*.
- Ask children to make notes and then orally retell the tale as a spooky story.
- Pick out a word or phrase you like, e.g. *He seems to sigh them still*. Write it down. In plenary, read out your choice and explain what you like about it, e.g. the sound, choice of word, the mood.
- Can you find a line that sounds noisy? One that sounds quiet? What sounds sound quiet? (Usually the letter *s* or other soft sounds.) Which letters make a noisy sound?

✍ Write

- **Whole-class activity: add a stanza using a writing frame.**
  - Attempt to add a stanza to the poem by completing the writing frame at the end of the workshop.
  - Subjects to start with might be:
    what the drinkers felt like when they heard the choir
    a fuller description of the drinkers following the ghostly choir
    the weather
    how the ghostly choir looked.
  - A rhyming dictionary can be of help. *The Penguin Rhyming Dictionary* is fairly easy to use. Use it to look up *night, pale, pane, dark*. Collect rhyming words and list them. Here are some of the words you might come up with: **night**, *white, moonlight, fright, sight, tight, plight, fight, might, mite;* **pale**, *frail, trail, sail, fail, stale, vale, veil, wail;* **pane**, *pain, lane, insane, train, wane, mane, main;* **dark**, *bark, park, lark, hark, stark*.
  - Use these words to help you to compose a stanza (or more!).
- **Move on to independent work.**
  - Individual children can rewrite the poem as a spooky story – using some of the vocabulary from the poem. Make notes of the story outline in the preparations.
  - The story can be brought up to date – retold in a contemporary setting.
  - The poem has the song-like structure of a ballad. The story can be retold as a modern song, for example as a rap or as a country-and-western song.
  - Retell a story you know as a ballad.

Perform! Discuss! Enjoy! Applaud!

Plenary and revision/redrafting

- Read out and comment on particularly good choices of words.
- Make the point that poems are worked and reworked. Can anyone suggest improvements or alternatives?
- Incorporate revisions.
- Ask children to write or type out their lines – with revisions incorporated. Present as a collection in Big Book or display format.

Possibilities for follow-up

Look at traditional ballads and other narrative poems. Make a collection or performance of them. Collect and read other poems by Thomas Hardy.

Objectives

This workshop is relevant to many year groups, particularly for the following objectives.

Y5T1 Text 6, 7, 9,12: read a number of poems by significant poets; analyse/compare styles of significant poets; develop active attitude towards reading; discuss enduring appeal of established/'classic' authors.

Y5T2 Text 3, 4, 5, 6, 12, 14: explore oral/written storytelling; read a range of narrative poems; perform poems in variety of ways; understand terms describing types of poetry; write extensions/additional verses for poems read; makes notes of story outline as preparation for oral storytelling.

Y5T3 Word 10, 11: understand how words can be formed from longer words; use a range of dictionaries effectively; Text 2, 6, 9: identify point of view; explore older literature; write in the style of the author.

Y6T1 Word 7, 10: understand how words/expressions have changed in meaning over time; understand function of etymological dictionary; Text 2, 3, 4, 5, 6: take account of point of view; articulate personal responses to literature; be familiar with work of established authors; contribute constructively to shared discussion about literature; manipulate narrative perspective (write in style of author; produce a modern retelling).

Y6T2 Word 7: understand that meanings of words change through time; Text 3, 5, 6, 9, 10: recognise how poets manipulate words; analyse moods/feelings in poems; discuss, interpret challenging poems; increase familiarity with significant poets of the past; use different genres as models to write.

Y6T3 Text 3: describe/evaluate style of particular poet.

Writing frame

The Dead Quire

You can approach this activity by doing the two rhyming lines first.

_____ (a)

_____ (b)

_____ (a)

_____ (b)

_____ (a)

The trees were black in the sky _____ (b)

_____ (a)

The wind was a distant sigh. _____ (b)

Here are some other lines to start you off.

The ground was white and hard with cold

The churchyard mossy, dank and old.

The choristers were ghastly pale

The air around them earthy stale.

Appendix

Mama Dot

Born on a Sunday
in the kingdom of Ashante

Sold on a Monday
into slavery

Ran away on Tuesday
'cause she born free

Lost a foot on Wednesday
when they catch she

Worked all Thursday
till her hair grey

Dropped on a Friday
when they burned she

Freed on a Saturday
in a new century

Fred D'Aguiar

An Anglo-Saxon Riddle

The wave, over the wave, a
weird thing I saw,

through-wrought, and
wonderfully ornate:

a wonder on the wave –
water became bone.

Anon.

From Beowulf

The hall of Heorot rang loud and
    long

With woe of warriors and grief of
    the great King.

Thereafter, from dark lake and
    dripping caves

Night after night over the misty
    moor

Came Grendel, gross and grim,
    famished for flesh.

Translated by Ian Seraillier

Figuratively Speaking

"Time to pull out all the stops,"

said the football coach.

"What do you mean?" I asked.

"Put your shoulder to the wheel," he explained,

"and your nose to the grindstone."

"What wheel? What grindstone?" I wondered.

"Keep your eye on the ball."

"I can do that," I said. "No problem."

"Chin up," he insisted. "Stiff upper lip."

I answered, "Mmmmmmmmmm." But it

was difficult to speak.

"Just hold your tongue, pull your socks up, hop to it and

put your best foot forward."

The coach blew his whistle.

"Argh!" I screamed,

as I tumbled in the mud.

The coach glared at me –

"Can't you follow a simple instruction?"

Michaela Morgan

November

No sun – no moon!

No morn – no noon –

No dawn – no dusk – no proper time of day –

    No sky – no earthly view –

    No distance looking blue –

No road – no street – no 't'other side the way' –

    No end to any Row –

    No indications where the Crescents go –

    No top to any steeple –

No recognitions of familiar people –

    No courtesies for showing 'em –

    No knowing 'em –

No travelling at all – no locomotion –

No inkling of the way – no notion –

    'No go' – by land or ocean –

    No mail – no post –

No news from any foreign coast –

No Park – no Ring – no afternoon gentility –

    No company – no nobility –

No warmth, no cheerfulness, no healthful ease,

    No comfortable feel in any member –

No shade, no shine, no butterflies, no bees,

    No fruits, no flowers, no leaves, no birds –

    November!

Thomas Hood

Recipe for a Story

Take an introduction.

Blend in atmosphere.

Stir in description and conversation.

Spice it up with suspense, humour, or
   adventure.

Allow to rise.

Cook thoroughly, checking it from
   time to time.

Add the finishing touches – a good
   final sentence.

Sprinkle with punctuation.

Serve piping hot.

Michaela Morgan